Where Beautiful Loves

Poetry and Prose

by

Brandy Lane

Fort Wayne, Indiana

© 2020 Where Beautiful Loves by Brandy Lane

Editor: Kindra M. Austin

All rights reserved.
Printed in the United States of America.

No part of this book may be used, stored in a system retrieval system, or transmitted, in any form or in any means—by electronic, mechanical, photocopying, recording, or reproduced in any manner whatsoever—without written permission from the author, except in the case of brief quotations embodied in critical articles and reviews.

Published in the United States of America by
Where Beautiful Inks LLC

Fort Wayne, Indiana

ISBN: 978-1-7363268-0-0

Library of Congress Control Number: 2020924708

Dedication

For my *dragon*,

my *maestro*,

my *darling pet*,

my *Leo*,

my *inimitable muse...*

my *friend*

whose name I will not tell,
but he knows who he is, very well.

You have given me the greatest gifts of all, unconditional love and friendship. You taught me to believe in myself again, and have encouraged me like no other. You will always be a mentor and someone that I look up to. I can only hope and pray that all of your dreams and aspirations come true. No matter where you go or where you end up, I will be cheering you on, praying for you and utterly happy just knowing you are somewhere on this planet with me. You are one of the best people that I know, and your example has caused me to change to become a better human. I wish you nothing but love, and success throughout your life and endeavors.

With every ounce of gratitude, friendship and love,

Brandy

Acknowledgments

With special thanks to my husband, Chris of twenty years, who has shown increasing love and support throughout this endeavor. He has been kind and helpful in setting up a quiet workspace for me, as well as bringing me tea and muffins when I forget to eat! He has shown tremendous understanding for me and my fantastical mind. I am most grateful that he has grown as a man, as a husband and as a father in the most tremendous ways in the past year and a half. It is amazing when you can watch a caterpillar morph into a butterfly, it can get messy at times, but with patience and perseverance, we have come through some of the rough patches of life. We still have a lot to learn about love and life, and are sometimes the example of what not to do, but we try our very best, and that is all we can ask of each other. We have learned that love comes in many forms, and that unconditional love can be shared with others. We've both gained an invaluable friend whom we love as family, and for this, I am eternally grateful.

I also want to thank my children, Maverick, Paisley, Daphne, and Broderick who are genuinely excited that I am following a dream. They have been kind and supportive, and a couple have even tried to write poetry themselves and follow me on Instagram. My greatest hope for each of them is that they are always true to themselves and work to follow their own dreams. Sometimes, I have to remember that their lives will be completely different from whatever expectations I might have for them, and that is great! They have taught me to love through adversity, and to fight for what I believe in. My children are going to be amazing adults someday, and I cannot wait to meet them.

Growing up, my brother and parents were always playing with words. We had fun with stories and rhymes and were always surrounded with music and open encyclopedias. I am grateful for the mythology and folklore, the religion and the puns. I'm grateful for the art and vacations, the science that was taught and explored. I grew to appreciate so very much, and love to the fullest capacity. Thank you, Mom and Dad and Chuck, for torturing me with word games and every pun on the planet.

I would like to thank my editor and friend, Kindra M. Austin, for her talents, and putting up with my very precise needs for this book. She is a wonderful human, not to mention patient. I am blessed to be able to work with her, as well as allowed to call her my friend.

Lastly, I am so grateful for my wonderful writing community on both Facebook and Instagram. Without your support, I probably wouldn't have gotten this far! I am very excited to have such great group to lean on and share encouragement. I would start listing names, but that might go for pages, and we need to get on to the real reason why we're all here… to read some poetry!

I am thankful to my Lord and savior, for all I have and being a beacon of hope even in the darkest of times, and for his greatest command;

> *"And now these three remain:*
> *Faith, Hope, Love,*
> *but the greatest of these*
> *is Love."*
>
> 1Corinthians 13:13

Contents

The Anticipation of Love
Expectant Heart 3
The Crush 4
Wonder 7
Antidote 8
Skeleton Key 12

From My Soul to Yours
Extracted 18
Soul Whisperer 20
Out 21
Kindred Souls 22
Destined 24
Affirmation 28
Grateful 32
Love Letter 36

Just a Tad Enamoured
That View! 42
Bloom 46
Silver Fox 51
Sticky, Sweet Words 52

Beautiful to Me 55
Not Going Anywhere 56
Worth 60
Mesmerized 62

Word Painting

Love 67
Paint My World 68
Masterpiece 76
Glittersick 78
Wearing Dusk 82
Humbled 84

A Universal Love

Atmosphere 90
White Hot 93
Ethereal 94
Universe 95
Transcendence 96
Essence of Time 97
Sun and Moon 98

The Roses and the Columbine

In the Garden 104
Rose Garden 107
Earthbound Angel 108

The Color of Falling 112
Magical 118
Where Beautiful Lives 120
Held 124

Unconditional
Oh. My. Goodness! 130
Enchanting 132
Dote 134
Forever Changed 136
Melt 139
Reminisce 140
It's You 142
Unrequited 144
Out Loud 146

The Mighty Dragon
Wellspring 154
Fly with Me! 156
My Darling Dragon 158
The Greatest High 162
Play with Me 164
Storytelling Dragon 166
Slumbering Dragon 167
Perspective 168

Wishes 170
Remind Him 172
Jump Start 174
A Sweet Hiraeth 179

Where Beautiful Loves

poetry and prose

My soul...

was but a tattered canvas, once beautiful with painted gardens and colorful butterflies...becoming faded and decrepit with neglect and abuse. The songs of my soul were all playing in minor, hauntingly lovely, yet utterly sorrowful. My heartstrings had been pulled out of tune.

My mind, a wasteland of burned out hopes and wanton dreams. An exhausted, hopeless, haze-filled chasm, incapable of comprehending my situation. I had grown to believe I would never be worthy of love, dignity, respect, admiration or loyalty. I was not much, and never enough...at least, that's what I believed.

Then I met him... He was like a mighty dragon, he mystified me and took me under his wing. A sounding board where I could bounce my chaotic thoughts, but when they landed back upon my ears, they sounded refined and orchestrated into perfect sense...I began to have confidence in my own voice again.

Every day I felt him course through my veins, never my lover, always my friend... but so much a part of me that he became intertwined with my soul.

It was instantaneous, the bond I felt with him like he was right there, inside of my mind... always keeping me company and giving me strength to get through every day. I gained courage, knowing I could stand up for myself... that I needed to in order to survive this world.

The Anticipation of Love

*The blushing coyness and curious mind of the possibilities of love.

Expectant Heart

My expectant heart
awaits the moment
I will catch your gaze.

I look away,

   blushing,

      contemplating

         how to breathe.

Oh, Calamity!
Oh, Trouble!
Why must these Earthly bounds
be so complicated?

Awaiting the day
when we can fly to the heavens,
where love can soar with no restraints.

No inhibitions,

love in its purest form
   as God intended it to be.

The Crush

This feeling has been dormant
for so very long,
like the permafrost in the Arctic.
Some moments, I feel lost
and unsure of my bearings.
Others, like a pent-up bolt of lightning.

My mind can't stay away,

no matter how I try

to keep you out.

Part of me wants to barricade every way in,
but I keep finding ways to peek out,
because I'm so undeniably curious.

I would donate my body to science
in order to understand
what is happening to me here!
So many songs,
poems,
written works
would say this is love...
or how they explain it to feel.

Where Beautiful Loves

I know it cannot be, however,
because it's impossible to love
someone you barely know.

Maybe it's pheromones...
but that cannot be,
because I am nowhere near you
ninety-eight percent
of the time.

I've questioned my sanity...
nope, only a bit outspoken,
but still all there.
Maybe I should get my head examined?
A tumor, some other anomaly?

Could it just be

an old-fashioned dose

of falling for you?

Oh dear.
I should run in the opposite direction,
but I am like a moth to a flame.

Brandy Lane

Mind over matter,
mixed with what seems like
the hormones of a teenage girl
with a crush on a pop star.

What makes you so enticing?
Why are you on my menu?

Part of me
wants you to set me straight...
the other part of me
wants to abandon
all of my wits and ravish you
like a lion that hasn't feasted for months.

Oh this is a travesty!
I am not myself as of late.
What is this unquenchable thirst,
this deep hunger?

There are no words!

Wonder

*I wish I could step into your mind...
just for a moment, you know, just to hear
the things that never leave your lips.*

I would love to see your thoughts
in their glorious colors,
and see the adventures
on imaginary trips.

Watching your face as you study mine,
as you listen intently to the words I share...
sometimes there's the slightest grin,
a look of wonder on there.

*I often wonder what's on your heart,
the things that you won't tell...*

the secret stories I'll never hear,
the mysteries never delved.

Maybe that's what makes you intriguing,
why you are my friend...
because I won't know where we're going
until we get to the end!

Brandy Lane

Antidote

Mystifying
how a mere nod from you
can cause such an
earth shattering response
within my soul.

Just a word,

    a smile,

        a glance

            in my direction.

Out of nowhere...
words flood my mind
and they trickle
down to my fingertips
to find their way to you.

It's an automatic response
that fills my heart
to overflowing.
Like the most
intoxicating view, or taste,
or touch, or fragrance,
my senses are heightened
to an otherworldly destination.

Where Beautiful Loves

My eyes glaze over,
my breathing deepens,
my mouth slightly waters
and I feel a comfortable
sense of warmth
and peace
in your presence.

What is this passion?
What is this insatiable quest
to be within your mind?

I often feel you hear me speak,

you feel me tremble,

you know my depth.

I must remind myself
that it's not possible,
that this is all in my own mind.

If just a few, mere printed words
can unleash this within me,

you cannot fathom

the amount of power

your gaze has.

Brandy Lane

You have an uncanny ability
to bring out the best in me.
My entire demeanor changes,
I stand taller,
my face lifts,

my world becomes a

    magical,

        beautiful,

           wonderful place

.................*when I remember*

....................*you*

......................*are in it.*

You don't even need
to be near me,
it's the mere essence
of you.

Where Beautiful Loves

I know not of how
you cast your spell,
or any antidote
for this feeling,
but if there were one…

I would refuse to take it!

I can't stop smiling.

Brandy Lane

Skeleton Key

Trying to keep
my eyes
wide open,
whilst muting
the din
of the world.

My mind

just wants

to play here

with you

for a while.

Meandering
into this peaceful
sanctuary,
where I'm safe
and cherished,
hoping
you'll take my hand
and just comfort me
for a spell.

Where Beautiful Loves

Resting here
brings me peace,
makes my burdens light,
carries me through.

*Your skeleton key
opened the depths
of my heart.*

Adoration

Thoughts of you
are gleefully distracting
my entire day!
I keep reminiscing about
your adorableness last night.
You cause me to be
dreamy,
and smiley,
and I cannot help but gush.
I am inebriated with
musings of you.

God must've had an amazing time creating you.

He gave you
such a compassionate heart,
a contagious laugh,
a brilliant mind,
an empathetic soul,
an uncontainable joy
and a perfectly dry wit...
mixed with the slightest hint
of sarcasm.
What a perfect cocktail!
You may be human,
but my goodness,
you are so much more to me!

From My Soul to Yours

*if my soul could speak, this is pretty much what it would say.

*I often feel
you hear me speak,
you feel me tremble,
you know my depth.*

Extracted

That sense of knowing,
where words
aren't needed anymore...

When we look through the windows

of these flesh and bone hovels

to gaze on each other's soul.

That is where my love
abounds for you...
not in mind and heart alone,
but transcending time,
and all that surrounds it.

Where history and future

combine with the present

and all I need is that one moment...

Just to be in your presence.

Where Beautiful Loves

I need nothing else
to make me happy!
Just having you here...
knowing you exist...
fills me with
incomprehensible joy!

My darling,

I cherish every word spoken,

every thought written,

every moment
I've spent with you

since the day we met.

I am flabbergasted
by this sweetness
that oozes from my fingertips...

my soul is extracted

onto paper,

for you.

Brandy Lane

Soul Whisperer

In the darkest hours of night,
just before the morning light...
I can hear you...
your soul speaking to mine,
telling me everything will be alright.

I feel a sense of comfort
as a smile eases across my face,
as if you've hugged me from within.

It's been awhile since I've heard you stirring...
but I'm glad you're back.

The missed hours of sleep are welcome
as long as my soul is with yours,
mingling...
even distance cannot erase this bond.

I know I'm loved,
you need not reassure me,

but it's always good to hear.

Out

My soul wants out...
rip open my chest,
tear into me...
It only wants to get to you.

My heart keeps

pounding...

pounding...

pounding...

trying to help it break free.

My thoughts wander...
they are rather fond
of one final destination...

you.

Brandy Lane

Kindred Souls

Some say beauty
is in the eye of the beholder,
but I must say that
it is in the heart!

Anything can be beautiful

to a heart

that has hope!

Even wild, untamed beasts
can be stunningly awesome
in the eyes of those who see
what they can become!

I used to see myself
as tired
and worn,
unworthy
and incapable
of being anyone
or anything of value.

When I looked into the mirror,
all I saw was a servant,
someone that was just here
to be kicked around.

Where Beautiful Loves

I don't ever want to be
in that place again.

You never saw me that way...
you have always valued me,

cherished me,

held me as precious.
You made me see
a completely different
reflection in the mirror.

I now have armor
for when I battle.

I have learned
to stand up and fight...
and am reminded that
somewhere on this planet,
I am loved by someone
in a way that no one else
has ever loved me.

My kindred soul,
my dearest friend...

it is you.

Brandy Lane

Destined

I've tried to restrain myself
for so long,
but I cannot tame
this heart of mine.

Time,
nor distance,
nor circumstance
changes the way I feel for you.
You are constantly with me,
you just are...

and I can't seem to push you
from my mind.
I've tried.

*It seems you are destined
to be one of those rare humans
whom I carry in my heart
until the day I no longer take breath...
and in my soul for even longer.*

Where Beautiful Loves

I long for you as though
you have been torn from me.

I need you as though I've lost you.

I love you as though you
are right within me,
and my heart is full of you.

You **embolden** me

to be the hopeless romantic
that I had forgotten I am.

You **enlighten** me

to seek knowledge
and wisdom continually.

You **emblazon** me

with desires and passion
and zeal for life, love, and for you.

You **embellish** me

with beauty and light,
and crown me as though I'm a princess.

Brandy Lane

I wish I could run to you!

This timing seems all wrong,
but all right at the same time.

I'm learning patience
as I have never known,
restraint and resilience as well.

I'm pouring my heart
into words that only come
when I am thinking of you,
and filled
with a passion unending.

All of the walls I have built up
don't even count with you,
as you've shattered the glass ceiling
to spend your time with me.

You flew in from above,
unexpected and serendipitously
you give freely to me,
although you go back to hide in your cave
shortly after.

Where Beautiful Loves

I so want to rescue you back!
I want to give to you as you have to me.

This is perhaps,
the most bittersweet,
most flavorful,
most enlightening,
most enchanting
of romances that I've ever known.

So utterly pure,
refined,
but bottled like the finest
and most rare of wines!

Part of me wants to break the seal and taste,
but everything in me says,

"not yet, wait until the perfect time".
It's so hard,
knowing that something so wonderful
awaits.

Affirmation

Oh the gorgeousness
of this day is exaggerated
by the glorious moments
I have spent in the mere
presence of you.

Your soul speaks
volumes to me,
sings ballads
and recites soliloquy.

I am filled with joy and light.

The light that you
have brought into my eyes,
my soul...
vanquished
the bitter cold and despair
that once consumed me.

Your gentle words,
your precious time,
your shoulder to cry on.

*You gave me a resting place,
when I had nowhere to go.*

Where Beautiful Loves

You nudged me
in the right direction
without touch,
and listened intently
to every word
that rolled off my tongue.

*You believed in me,
even when I doubted myself...*

and you even chased
those demons right away.
You constantly protect me,
even though I never asked.
You watch from afar
and allow me to be myself.

You allow me to freely love you,
with no boundaries or rules.
I dote on you
and lavish you with praises
that you might think
are undeserved,
but I see you,
I know your soul,
your pureness
and transparency.

Brandy Lane

You will always be
a part of me,
I feel you everywhere I am.
I long to spend time with you,
even if just in thought.

I cannot imagine
my life without you now,
nor do I want to.

It would be

like the night

without the stars,

the day

without the sun.

Where Beautiful Loves

My brain
makes
love
to you
in words,
and seeks
every moment
to steal
kisses
through
small quips
and daydreams!

Grateful

Your exuberance excites me!

*You make me want to shine
like the stars in the night sky.*

Brilliance within the darkest depths of stillness
in the far reaches of the universe.

I want to compose the greater picture with you.
Where every nerve of every sense is touched
through song and artistry.

Where beauty is felt and not just seen.

I want to ignite the passion, spark love
and ingenuity, reaching into the hearts and souls
of all who are willing to hear and give them
that passionate, harmonious joy
that I have within my own.

My dear, you have given me more
than any human on this planet ever has.
I can feel again, I can breathe again,
my tears are no longer for pain, but for joy.
You've given me confidence, hope, acceptance…

Where Beautiful Loves

I am like an unpolished, but brilliant diamond,
and I look forward to working with you
to hone the edges and polish the facets.

You can make me shine even more.
I am yours as long as you'll teach me.

The mere mention of my name from your lips still bathes me from head to toe in comfort. You make me feel absolutely stunning!

I adore you for your beautiful mind,
your charming wit, and your subtle awkwardness.
I want to be the cherub in your ear,
cheering you on, and reminding you
that you are so much more than what the world
tries to limit you to.

Thank you for seeing my hidden parts
and bringing them to light.
You've always seen right through me...
the things you've said.
You've sucked me in, I'm smitten!
You are such a mystery, and I'm swept up in you.

Brandy Lane

Having you in my life is like reading the most fabulous, intense book and never wanting to put it away.

You are better than sleep, better than food...
I can't put you down!

I will mourn when the book is over,
but at the same time,
take every experience with me
throughout my entire life.

As for now,

I look so forward to the coming chapters!
I never knew I could write so intensely.
You've unearthed a talent
that only you have the key to.

Oh please don't ever
completely leave my life…
even the mere trickle
of your replies
waters these desert sands
and brings forth
blooming flowers.

Brandy Lane

Love Letter

My heart breaks daily
as it falls in love with you
over and over again.

You are the first person
I wish to say good morning to,
and my last thought of the night
as I close my eyes.
Every time get good news
or sad news,
you are the one I run
to share it with.

You are the one I wish to hold
when I'm happy
or when I need to be consoled.
You're my dearest love!

You are my home,
and I have been away from you
for far too long.

I wish to open the door
to your infectious smile
and see that beloved
twinkle in your eye.

Where Beautiful Loves

*I found you,
and my life
irrevocably changed in ways
I never knew it could.*

All of the magic came back...
the creative,
colorful,
wonderful
beauty of life.

The love that I carry
courses through these veins...
it keeps me going forward,
gives me the strength
to face the demons every day.

I will not give up knowing
you are on the other side.

I ask that you bear with me,
for this battle will be long
and weary.

Brandy Lane

*Our time on Earth is so short
compared to the moments
my soul has known you,
that depth is countless!*

Just a Tad Enamoured

*I may have blushed a little when I wrote these...

Whenever I am lonely, I just think of the way one side of your mouth curls into a smile ahead the other... then I'm smiling, because somehow, you're right there with me.

Brandy Lane

That View!

I dare not address you
by your first name
until properly invited,
but such a beautiful one it is!

To say it aloud is almost
an appreciative sigh
of the entire body.
Relaxing, intriguing,
dreamy even...

*I stopped myself
from sending this last evening,
until I was of proper wit.*

(One glass, I swear!)

I've decided that it's just
too high a compliment
not to send,
and I am hoping
that you will just accept it
as my appreciation of
His creation before me.

Where Beautiful Loves

He is,

after all,

the divine artist.

Oh my!
(you might want
to close the door,
as I can imagine
you'll blush
and laugh
just a little abruptly
from shock and awe.)

I, after all,
gasped slightly
and my eyebrow cocked
as I took in the view.
Blushing now,
even the thought,
as I would staring
at any great work.

Oh, why couldn't we
have been born
in the same time,
centuries ago?!

My musings
would be among
those studied as those
of the greatest love prose!

I would've been famed for my slight obsessions of you!

Here goes…

A slight intoxication
from the vine,
and my thoughts turn
to only you.

Slightly inappropriate even,
but my goodness!

Where Beautiful Loves

*The view
when you are walking away!*

If you could see what I see,
you would understand!

*I can only liken it
to the experience of gazing
at the backside of
Michelangelo's "David".*

And, there it is.
Really,
no response is necessary
(seriously,
just don't reply).
I just wanted you to know
that whether you're coming...
or going,
the view is
spectacular!

Bloom

I'm going to do it...
sigh,
I'm going to type
your beautiful name!

Wait!

Maybe I'm being too forward,
maybe you will be offended!
I always try to be respectful…
as you have earned your title.

Oh, but your name is so gorgeous to me!

It elicits the same feelings
of everything in bloom,
the sun bursting forth
in glorious day,
the pines reaching
toward the moon at night,
the streams rushing forth
with the fresh snowmelt
from the mountains.

Where Beautiful Loves

You make the dullness
of this world fade away.

In a world
where small courtesies
are mostly abandoned,
I feel so respectful toward you.

How do you do that?

Maybe it's in the way you say mine...

Like you are holding a
precious jewel.

You speak it with utmost care
and caress every letter as it rolls
off your tongue.

You say it as though I'm important,
and worthy, and without disdain.

You show me a respect
that I am probably deserving of,
but haven't been shown
in a very long time.

Brandy Lane

Isn't it amazing
how one little act of eloquence
can touch someone so deeply?

Oh, this connection
is like none I've ever felt!
*I love the way I stumble a little
when I first see you.*

All of these words
that are built up inside of me,
kind of fall into a jumble
when you are near,
like a scrabble bag
waiting for a hand
in finding the next letters
to form words.

On one hand,
you make me a beautiful princess,
a writer,
a rose in bloom...
on the other,
a bumbling idiot
with absolutely no wits about me.

Where Beautiful Loves

It's exhilaration unleashed,
never knowing
what I'm going to say
to your gorgeous face,
with those glittering blue eyes,
and mischievous grin,
that is If I can garner the courage...

It's like trying to peek at sun!
Oh for heaven's sake,
I've gone overboard again!

And as much as I want
to type your name,
I will wait.

I would rather
hold this anticipation
until I can whisper it
from my lips
to your ear
and give it the proper intonation

It needs to be spoken
with the fire
and passion
and energy behind it
that I feel every time I think of you.

Brandy Lane

My friend,

you are so worthy of that respect,

thank you

for showing graciousness to me.

I'm so grateful for you.

Where Beautiful Loves

Silver Fox

You referred to yourself as *"grandpa"*...
I'd say you're a silver fox!
Soft and fluffy or slick and tamed,
with gorgeous, glittery locks.

Sparkling eyes that show compassion,
along with a sly, nearly naughty grin...
that slowly creeps into a smile,
just above that strong, handsome chin.

Your tall stature is comforting,
like a place I've never been...
I just want to stay awhile
and curl up, your arms within.

Your hands are strong and wide,
and can hold so much more than mine...
yet I marvel at your gentleness,
your soul is none but kind.

Your mind is constantly creating,
never staying still...
unlike what we see on the outside,
sometimes muted, if you will.

A gentleman even when facetious...
I'm not sure how you do it.
All I know is that I'm privileged
to be akin to it.

Brandy Lane

Sticky, Sweet Words

You have done it again.
Your
sticky,
   sweet
      words have glued themselves
permanently in my mind where they
play
   like
      a song to my soul.

Each wonderful little compliment,
sent on
little
   angel
      wings to help restore
my confidence and
heal
   my
      heart.

Where Beautiful Loves

You cover me in feathers, as

each

   sweet

      essence lands on me,
lifts me to soaring heights,
then ever so gently,

brings

   me

      back to softly land on my feet.

You make me beautiful, you

adorn

   me

      in gold and make my rough edges
something to wear as though
I should not be ashamed,
but wear them proudly as

crowned

    jewels.

You make me

strive

  to

    succeed...

I love to learn,
and you make me

a

  little

    competitive in this way!
I am pleasantly surprised
at how many things
your influence has

brought

  to

    my life!

Beautiful to Me

Sometimes I can't help
but stare…
I love to look at every
fleck in your eyes,
the glints of sparkles
popping up in your hair.

The adorable dimples
that appear when you smile…
the little creases under your eyes
when you work too hard and are tired.
You are a masterpiece,
a work of art.

I could marvel for hours
and never grow weary.

You are breathtakingly beautiful to me.

Brandy Lane

Not Going Anywhere

You have said
you aren't going anywhere.
That is so profound in my mind.

I'm so used to being a caged bird
that I can't wait to fly.

I so want to make a home
in your branches,
as you already give me
respite from the storms.

You are such an unwavering,
strong,
intelligent being.
When I think of you,
I see you as a mighty tree,
never bending to the winds,
but still lofty enough
to let your delicate leaves
feel the breeze.

Where Beautiful Loves

You fight for what you believe in,
and learn everything you can
to better yourself.
Constantly studying,
dreaming,
working toward a goal.

Who are You?

You are like a river bend,
swift and clear,
deep and cool,
lapping at the grasses
as you sweep by.

Home to many
who come to lay on your banks
and refresh themselves
within your waters.

Brandy Lane

You are like a cottage in the wilderness,
a cozy home
with a fire always lit
to welcome the weary wanderer.

You elicit emotions

from my hidden places,

a vehemence

which I have never known.

Unlocking gated alcoves
of my mind and heart.

I ask again, as I have before.
Who are you?
From whence have come to me?
I know not which way to go,
for you speak to me without words
as no one ever has.

Where Beautiful Loves

I want to compose the greater picture with you. Where every nerve of every sense is touched through song and artistry. Where beauty is felt and not just seen. I want to ignite the passion, spark love and ingenuity. Reaching into the hearts and souls of all who are willing to hear and give them that passionate, harmonious joy that I have within my own.

Worth

I am constantly compelled
to explain your worth,
I'm not sure why...
and only God knows
the purpose in all of this,
but all I know is
that you being in my life
is something
I desperately needed.

I do so wish I could

hear the intricate,

intimate thoughts

in your mind.

I never truly know
what you're thinking
underneath
that wonderful head of hair.

Where Beautiful Loves

I do know that
your eyes
twinkle more now
than they used to,
and that you seem
more open and upbeat.

I dare not take credit...
but it does leaves me

to wondering...

Mesmerized

I am enveloped in sweetness,
doused in dripping,
lingering thoughts of you.
I try to abstain,
but you're like the rarest,
most decadent treat!
It's hard to push you away,
I crave you more and more.

You are such a radiant being,
so demure
and calm in your demeanor.

You are most fascinating
to watch when you direct,
as you dance with the notes
and mesmerize us
with your movements.
I am under your spell,
and don't ever wish to be let go.

You truly are a masterpiece,
and I could stare and critique
for hours
and not find a single flaw.

Where Beautiful Loves

In my eyes, you are perfection;
from the glittering hair on your head
to your untied shoelaces…
your Michelangelo's backside
and your sparkling eyes,
your mischievous grin
and your strong, downy covered arms.

I'm probably just some
pebble in your shoe with all
of the bothersome ways
I've planted myself in your life.

I'm not quite sure
if I'm a blessing or a curse!
All I do know is that

I can't bear the thought

of being without you.

You are a constant
in my heart and mind,
and it's a feeling that never dulls.

Word Painting

*where my thoughts come alive on paper.

Love

The rage... the hurt.

Must love torture the lives of those who discover its sweetness?

Does true passion ever exist purely,
or is it something we chase?
A dream that expires upon waking
to the realities of life?

These are my greatest questions,
for the elixir of love has intoxicated many
and caused harm...
are there any truly happy endings?

Brandy Lane

Paint My World

*If I could only lasso all
of my drifting thoughts
with a pen
and ensnare them
in the fibers of paper!*

There are so many,
some small and fleeting,
some so overwhelming
that I can't even consider!

Oh, I'm so dramatically
filled with disdain!

In one part of my mind...
I have to envision
a little sheepdog
gathering the culprits
and corralling them away!

It's as if certain people in life
carry around buckets of dull,
gray paint and are hell bent
on covering up any beauty that exists!

Where Beautiful Loves

Every day,
I gather my tools;
a brush,
some beautiful paints...
each color representing
things that bring joy.

I repaint the world

little by little,

exactly how

I like it to be.

I live there,
and invite people in often.
Some people visit,
or just observe,
some stay for quite some time.

Then there are some
that are only there
to destroy all that I live for
or love
or dream about
with no regard
to my painstaking work,
my heart
or soul.

Brandy Lane

No appreciation,
just wanting to take
what they want,
and leave a torn,
worthless canvas behind.

*I'm exhausted
of that part of my life!*
How can one renovate
one room in a building
that is condemned?
It is not structurally sound!

I could slap paint up
all I want,
and add decorations
and plant flowers...
and it won't ever fix the foundation.

I don't even know if it's fixable!
I could move
the crumbled concrete
and find a sink hole underneath
for all I know.

Where Beautiful Loves

I am discouraged in trying
to make something grow
where nothing seems
sustainable.

Yet, I am constantly compelled to try.
I have to switch gears here,
my heart is so heavy today,
but I share only because
you help me paint.

I hand you a brush,

and you come along side me.

You've colored my days

and my nights are full

of beautiful dreams.

My muse...
you have been gracious
to allow me to adventure with you
by being my pet dragon,
my maestro,
my hero
and my friend.

Brandy Lane

You stepped in
when my prayers
had nearly ceased
and my light
had nearly faded.

You've tolerated
my cheesiness,
laughed with me
at my awkwardness,
and have held
my proverbial hand
along the way back
to who I am meant to be.

You have reminded me

that I am talented,

beautiful,

one of a kind,

and much more intelligent

than I let on.

I know
that none of this
was intentional,
but you,

Where Beautiful Loves

just allowing me
to express
everything I am to you
has changed my world.

It couldn't have been

with anyone

other than you.
You,
my angel,
are absolutely beautiful
to me.

This human form
is so awkward to me...

In my mind
and heart
I am so close to you,
but even in the same room,
I still cannot be
as carefree with you
as I am on paper.

These earthly binds
of flesh
and bone
constrict in ways
I cannot explain.

Where Beautiful Loves

If my soul
could dance with yours
but for a moment!
Who needs wine
when intoxication comes
with the mere thought
of your presence?

Oh, never stop painting my world!

I never even knew
I needed you,
and now I know
that I don't want
to be without.

You paint my world.

Brandy Lane

Masterpiece

*If I could pour
my liquid thoughts of you
onto a canvas,
it would be
the most glorious painting
ever created.*

Priceless,
renowned,
highly sought after.

If I could fill page
after page
with words describing
every small detail of you,
and how wonderful
you make my world,
it would fill enough books
to fill every library on this earth,
and I would still have
plenty more to say.

Where Beautiful Loves

You have made me
so much more
than who I had become.

You are my missing piece.

I was utterly and completely
on the way to the junk pile
when you picked me up
and saw my worth!
You've shined me
with encouraging words,
put a spring in my step,
gave me hope,
saw right through to
my very passionate core.

I swear,

you see right through me.

You have made me priceless,
where I was worthless.
You have helped to uncover
a masterpiece.

Brandy Lane

Glittersick

The effervescence...
the bubbly way
you make me feel
just thinking about you.

The satiny sheen
my skin glows
when I'm intoxicated
with thoughts… of you.

You make me see stars

on the cloudiest of nights,

and rainbows when

there's not a drop

of rain to be found.
Dew drops
in the morning
reflect the shimmering rays
of the sun.
Refracting beams bounce
off of the stream
outside of my window,
landing playfully
on the ceiling
above my bed.

Where Beautiful Loves

I lie there,
watching them dance...
much like the sparkles
in your eyes.

Sigh...
to breathe in
the same air that has been
inspired
and expired by you...
to be in the presence
of your soul,
with its brilliance
and glorious illumination...
that is the most glorious
closeness
I can imagine.

Everywhere I look,
I see you...
no matter how much I try,
I cannot extract you
from my thoughts!

Brandy Lane

You
have somehow
placed yourself
in every crevice
of my mind...
much like
the glitter
all over my home
after the holidays.

You

are a constant reminder

of gifts

and love

and everything

that encompasses

elation!

I crave it,
I need it,
I'm loving
each sparkle I see
for it reminds me
of you.

Where Beautiful Loves

When you are not near,
and I can't find the light...
I feel a though
I'm missing my essence,
my purpose,
as though I'm missing home.

You are my inspiration,

my sanctuary,

my hearts and minds' desire!
There is only one word
that I can even fathom
to call this loss
when you are not in my presence...

"Glittersick"

Wearing Dusk

Your gaze falls upon me
like the sunset upon a weary days end,
your eyes meet mine,
and I know you are
undressing me
slowly
in the twilight.

You strip me of all of my inhibitions,
there is nothing I cannot say
or think
or do,
here in the safety of your arms.

You take my insecurities...
one by one,
and toss them aside,
touching my soul in the ways
that only you can.

Where Beautiful Loves

You intently look at me as though
I'm the most brilliant diamond
you've ever seen,
you smile at my beauty,
shining from within.

You crown me with respect,
and I feel like a princess in a beautiful gown,
even though I'm only cast
in the waning rays of light.
You love me
with the glaring light of day,
even when
I'm only wearing dusk.

Brandy Lane

Humbled

I suppose I never noticed
the sheer amounts of
gold that surrounded me
until the moment you
came into my life.

The rays of sun
in various times of the day,
the leaves in the fall,
the daffodils in the spring,
the dandelions in the summer.

The fields of gold
that surround the land where I live,
in dry grasses
or in sunflower fields.

I suppose that I started
to treasure
the things around me a little more,
just because I had you
to share them with.

Where Beautiful Loves

I know that nothing in this life
is permanent,
but as long as I have breath,
I will remember you fondly
even if you forget about me.

In the short time
you have been in my life,
you changed the entire course
of where I was going.

You changed
the way that I think,
the way that I learn,
the way that I interact with others.

I have never been

so enchanted by another,

nor so inspired.

I will forever be humbled
by knowing you.

You make me feel
important,
and so very loved.
It doesn't even matter if the
world turned against me…
I have one person
who deems me worthy.

A Universal Love

* A Love that Transcends Space and Time

Thinking of you
has become like breathing...
continuous and automatic.
When I try to stop doing
either,
I feel as though
I'll shrivel up and die!

Brandy Lane

Atmosphere

The essence
of all that you are
is like a puff of smoke!
A mist that vanishes
as quickly
as it comes,
out of seemingly,
nowhere.

A spirit,
an orb of energy,
a cosmic,
nuclear blast...
blinding
and demolishing
anything
that was there
prior.

What are we made of
that each atom
within my being
moves
when I'm near you...
drawing me in
like a black hole?

Where Beautiful Loves

This magnetism
with forces
that are beyond
my control?

Nebulae, entwined
in a heavenly glow...
the combined energy
of a million stars!

My soul, when it collides

with yours...
shatters every wall
I've ever built,
any barrier.

I know you can see
right into my soul...
I've seen you

stare
right into
my very core.

Brandy Lane

Meteors streak down
hot,
and fast
and bright,
like the thoughts
that speed
through my mind,
not quite knowing where
they are going
to land.

It doesn't ever really matter,
because they seem to
burn right up
in your atmosphere...
and sometimes,

I wonder

if you even got to see

my thoughts

at all...

Where Beautiful Loves

White Hot

White hot
and never fading,
it's nuclear…
producing
an energy all its own.

You see,

that's the thing

about love,

the truer it is,

the more wild,

untamable,

atomic

and blinding it is.

The energy
of ten thousand suns
are pent up
in this sacred universe
within my heart!

Brandy Lane

Ethereal

My bond with you is ethereal,
otherworldly, fantastical
and heavenly all at once.

The universe could birth
an entire galaxy within the energy
that I feel when I am around you,
and stars for every thought.

You've done nothing to pull me in,
it's not your fault!
I don't know where
you are supposed to fit!

I want to run away
and explore the nooks and crannies
of life through your eyes,
but you know that I am bound.
You allow me to dream,
to hope,
to strive for more.

Where Beautiful Loves

Universe

You simultaneously have me
with my head in the clouds,
my feet on the ground
and my heart in your hands.

The comfort I feel with you

is my favorite feeling

in the universe.

Caught between
cozy and squishy,
beauty and passion,
fire and light...
that feeling of seeing
the Northern lights,
a majestic lightning bolt
as it streaks across the sky...
that magnetic
and electric energy.

Transcendence

Even in death,
I would write you poetry...
hoping it would transcend
the heavens to you.

Should I be your angel,
I would send you gifts
to brighten your every day...
a nudge from your cat,
a beautiful flower,
a shooting star...
singing birds
and the fragrance
of a mountain breeze.

I would find the things
that comfort you,
and wrap you in them,
always to cheer you.
My heart wields a love
I've never experienced before.
It never ebbs,
just overwhelms my soul.
I try and tame it, keep it caged,
but it melts the bars
and conquers the demons
that try to contain it.

Essence of Time

Sigh, but the minutes
ooze like hours…
like lava toward the shore,
slowly growing immovable
as it turns to rock.

There to stay,
building upon itself
until there are islands,
is the essence of the time
in which I wait to spend time
with my dearest friend.

Oh! Chaos
and distorted rhythms
of the continuum!

Why do moments
seem like millenniums
when you are not with me,
but shoot like meteors
in the night sky,
burning out so quickly
when you are-
making me question
their existence at all?

Brandy Lane

Sun and Moon

If I could

capture the *sunshine*,

I would place it outside your window...
to brighten your days and disposition.

As far as the *moon*?

I'd put a pull chain on it so you could
turn it off when you wanted to see

all of the *stars*...

and turn it on

whenever you felt alone at *night*.

You could adjust it waxing or waning,
so you could take a midnight stroll,

or sit quietly next to your *true love*
and watch it move across the night sky.

And although she couldn't see him, she knew that he was there, just like the moon in the sky when it is new.

She saw the stars and made a wish, in hopes to see him soon.

The Roses and the Columbine

*all that is lovely in the garden...

If I could only
take your pain
as easily as autumn's kiss
banishes the green from the
leaves...
I would kiss your cheeks
until you blushed like a
crimson maple!

Brandy Lane

In the Garden

I'm stealing time
to drink in the moment,
to find that refreshing spring
that gushes forth
the essence of you...

The place
where my body and soul refill
to find peace and light, and comfort...
where all the pain fades
and I am whole...

The place where angels
lift me up on wings
to reach the words
as they tumble from your lips
so that I may find the meaning
in everything you say...

You give me so much joy,
so much ecstasy
in this realm of literary abundance.
I can pick and choose
anything I desire,

as if I were Eve in the garden.

Where Beautiful Loves

As bright red cherries
and sweet dark plums
are ever in abundance...

I dare not taste the apples!

As ruby red
and shiny they may be,
and how I long
for the refreshing juice
as I would sink my teeth
into their crisp flesh,

I dare not go near them!

So tempting as they are...
the tart, yet sweet scent
and wonderful shape
will have to be ignored!

As your lips,
as full and succulently sweet
entice me with every word you say,

I must avert my eyes

so as not to be tempted

to take even the smallest taste!

Brandy Lane

I am left thirsty and hungry...
licking my lips, subconsciously, wishing...

Oh! This unquenchable desire
taunts me and rocks me to my core!
I must abstain... but in my mind,
I cannot stay away!

I will just have to visit the garden,

and your lips in thought only.

Rose Garden

You aren't just a rose,
my darling,
you are the entire garden!

From the tender roots
and fertile soil,
to the branches,
buds
and flowers.

From the shiny leaves
and tiny mushrooms,
to the blooms
of every sort.

Every color,
fragrance,
texture,
fruit
and honey bee.

Everything working
together
to make you
as wonderfully complex
as you are!

Brandy Lane

Earthbound Angel

Your smile dissolves
my dark and cold
landscape
into liquid
sunshine...
and flowers
bloom
in the depths
of my heart.

Brilliant colors
are everywhere
that gloomy grays
once covered.

Despair,
chaos,
and hatred
give way to

peace,

hope

and love.

Where Beautiful Loves

Calm,
beautiful
enunciation of words
that pour
from your lips,
are made thick
and deep
and beautiful
like honey
from the rarest
and most
exotic flowers.

The
sing-song
of your voice
lulls me into a trance
as you speak,
and takes me
into a place
that is safe,
where I am
cherished

and where the *Lord* knows

my name.

Brandy Lane

God
has given me
an earthbound angel
for a short time.
I cannot fathom
what I will do
when my time with you
comes to
an end.

Such a short time
to relish
in the presence
of your songs,
wrapped in your music,
bathed in your light.

Where Beautiful Loves

I am comforted
in knowing that,
although we may have to part,
it isn't an eternal separation.

I will get to

play

and sing,

laugh

and smile,

and curl up

under your wings

again someday.

And then,
I will praise
the Lord with you
for all eternity.

Brandy Lane

The Color of Falling

Weightless,
yet feeling the depth
and the weight
of the world,
the pressure
inside of this chasm.

Moments
last forever,
replayed
in my mind,
all of my thoughts
of you...

Crimson
are the roses,
the blooming

love

inside of my heart,
my soul,
my blossoming mind
erupts
in wildflowers
covering
the once-barren
landscape of these bones
in brilliant colors.

Where Beautiful Loves

My cheeks
blush in
pink
as I catch

your gaze.

Persimmon
are the day lilies
standing tall and upright,
swaying
as I do
when engaging in conversation
with you.

The light of evening
shining through my
auburn hair,
as the
tangerine sun
sets slowly in the West.

Canary,
is the brilliant light
that wakes me in the morning,
reminding me

that today is a new day
to dote upon you.

I daydream
of walking through fields of
gold
with you
(as I absentmindedly
burst the
saffron
bubble
of the yolk of my eggs.)

Evergreen,
is the love
that grows inside of
my heart,
never changing
with the seasons.
The ivy winding
through my veins,
peeking through the cracks
that others have made
within my soul...
my love for you
has no bounds.

Cerulean
are your twinkling eyes,

Where Beautiful Loves

full of amazement
and affection
for me,
seeing into
my murky soul.

*The midnight blue
of the sky,
fills with stars,
they represent
every thought
I have of you.*

Periwinkle
are the galaxies,
with hints of
heliotrope
and streaks of
violet.
Those far off
destinations
where I can transcend
in thoughts,
my longing to escape

Brandy Lane

with the one I love.

I've fallen to the point
where I can fly.

*When you walk
into the room,
your love
shines
through the darkness,
igniting the
fires of my heart.*

Light shines brightly
through the prisms
that surround my soul,
like diamonds
sparkling in the sun.

Just look into my eyes
and you will see
the colors of falling...
for you.

Where Beautiful Loves

It would be heaven if I could just simply hold you for a little longer, gaze into your beautiful eyes and get to soak in everything about you.

Brandy Lane

Magical

Words tossed through the air
from my lips to you,
careful not to bruise you
in any way...

Like soft feathers,
land on your head softly,
comforting
and warm.

Wishing to console,
uplift and caress your ego
ever
so slightly, as to remind you
of how amazing you are.

Waking your senses,
one by one,
and dousing you
with everlasting love.

Pouring out compliments
as perfumed oils
that dance on your skin
before readily absorbed.

Your many talents
entice and enthrall
as I sit in wonderment

Where Beautiful Loves

of your fantastic, genius mind.

If only the world
could see what I see,
how beautiful a being
you are!

If they'd just sit a moment and meander in the gardens inside your skull.

The symphonies,
scenarios, mystical things
you've made up
in your mind!

The things replayed,
bringing past reality to life
so that others can live on
from the not so distant past...

You are like a portal
to realms undiscovered,
music yet to be written.

You are magical.

Brandy Lane

Where Beautiful Lives

I cannot push you from my mind.
I simply cannot hide you away!

I've tried,
but just the mere thought of you
curls my frown into a smile.

I cannot find words to write anyone but you!
Everything else is seemingly, garbage...
with no tenderness or thought.

For you, however, the words just melt
onto the blank backdrop of the screen.
I can say just about anything to you here,
and know that you will be comforted,
as I am in knowing you are reading my thoughts.

I escape to the heights of my imagination...
walking with you in fields of gold,
you look down at my face
to brush the hair from my cheek.

I stare into those ocean eyes
and get lost at sea.

Where Beautiful Loves

You are where beautiful lives!
You are where kindness reigns!
You embolden me in every way.

I say these words
not to flatter you in any way,
as I have nothing to gain...
but to express just how much
you are to me.

You may think
I give you too much credit,
and it is all in my imagination...

but, my dear, it only takes
one spark
to light a fire...
and you've got me ablaze
with hope and desire.

Where Beautiful Loves

It is you that my heart longs for,
it is you that I adore...
as hard as that has been for me to admit,
that is where I am.

No matter what,
whether love blooms here,
or just a beautiful friendship...
that won't change the fact
that I will be continually
tending this garden.

It's rather exciting,
not knowing what will spring forth...
just as long as there are no pesky weeds!

I will always be here for you,
come hell or high water.

*You mean too much to me
to not have you in my life.*

I have made that abundantly clear.
I'm learning a lot from you,
boundaries being one great lesson,
as no one ever showed me respect in that sense.
I, in return...
respect you.

Brandy Lane

Held

Wild roses and columbine
bloom in the craggy depths
and rocky crevices
in the circumstances
that keep me from you.

Nothing but beauty grows
in the vacuum of time
we are held captive within.

Every second,

however slowly it passes,

brings blossoming gardens

where an empty chasm

was once beheld.

Although music halls
are emptied,
and floating melodies
cannot freshly linger in the air,
the songs of my heart
still dance with memories of you.

Where Beautiful Loves

I may be distanced physically
by time and circumstance,
but my heart and mind are always
right there with you.

I am comforted in the mystery,
because I know the prize
at the end of this sequester
is to be once again in your arms...
safe and loved,
precious and adored...
as I already am in your heart.

Unconditional

*sigh

I long to see your dancing eyes, and feel the rush of blood to my cheeks as I catch your gaze.

Brandy Lane

Oh. My. Goodness!

I so wish I could see you
before you must leave...
if for no other reason than
to throw my arms around you
one more time
and watch your mouth curve
into that wonderful smile!

I absolutely adore your face
when your dreamy eyes glance my way
and you unabashedly just slightly simper...

Oh. my. goodness!

My brain makes love to you in words, and seeks every moment to steal kisses through small quips and daydreams!

This is a most glorious start to my day,
and I would simply be content,
musing of you.

Where Beautiful Loves

*I absolutely,
without a doubt,
with every part of me...
love you.*

This is certainly
a love like none I've ever known...
as there is not one prerequisite,
nothing required of you,
no regulations, no judgment...
much rather like the closest thing
to how I imagine
the purest form of loving to be,
completely unconditional.

You strengthen my very soul,
and I feel more complete
just knowing you are there.

Brandy Lane

Enchanting

My beloved,
even in the stillness
of the world at this moment,
my heart steadily beats
in its enchanting rhythm...
calling for you.

Love pulses through my veins
with no final destination...
writing down these emotions
are my only release.

Shall I never get the chance
to whisper into your ear
or glide my fingers
through your hair?
To hold you in my arms?

My glorious love,
I long to be
within your presence,
as I am never fully satisfied
in the days that are not
spent with you.

Where Beautiful Loves

*You
are my favorite
place to be,
still my home
away from home...*

How much longer
must I be without?

Oh, I shall not
squander these days
nor fetter my feelings,
but instead,
relish in this love I have...
only for you.

Why shouldn't I?

For it is the
most wonderful feeling
I have ever known,
and I shall cherish it
for a lifetime.

… Brandy Lane

Dote

Dost thou not love me anymore...
do you not think of me?
It is something that I must implore
please put my mind at ease!

I miss knowing that my doting
is causing that slight simper...
Just a crumb, a little taste,
please don't make me whimper!

I miss the banter back and forth
the closeness that we've shared,
I fear the lack of seeing you...
has left my heart impaired!

Oh please tell me you've missed me...
Just a little bit?
My silliness, my smile,
my awkwardness, my wit?

I've missed you mercilessly,
I've discovered as I pondered,
thinking how much you mean to me...
through memories I've wandered.

Where Beautiful Loves

*You are someone that I choose to know
as long as I have breath.
You are someone that I choose to love...
with unhindered height and depth.*

I only know that in my mind,
you are a part of me...
and if you ever need someone,
here, forever I will be.

Brandy Lane

Forever Changed

You always leave me wondering...
I think it's how you ensnare!

You're mysterious,
and that is intriguing to me.
Leaving tidbits,
but never the whole story.

There is certainly no
skipping to the end
to see what happens with you,
is there?

Nerve wracking,
confusing,
bewildering,
mystifying...

Sometimes I wonder

if you're real

or just a figment

of my imagination!

Where Beautiful Loves

I can only contemplate
scenarios in my head
as to how you will take me.

On one side of the coin,
I recognize everything about you...
you are comfortable
and familiar,
you are everything I could ask for
in another human...

Your soul,
your essence,
your wit.

On the flip side,
I know absolutely
not one iota
about you.

Less than a paragraph,
really.

What's underneath
your candy coating?

What makes you tick?

What's important to you?

Brandy Lane

I can tell you what I see
until the cows come home...
maybe I see more than most?

I do know
that I'm still ever
so fascinated by you,
my nightingale,
my sweet fragrance,
my breath of fresh air!

I still know not
from whence you came.

I do know that
I am forever changed
just by your presence
on this planet,
even in the
brief time
I've known you.

I also know that
I don't want
to ever be
without you,
whatever that looks like.

Melt

Meandering thoughts
give me
moments of relief
with glimpses of hope.

Memories
dance around more quickly,
morphing
my frown into a grin.

Melancholy
gives way to a giggle,
as mischievously,
my simper widens.

Miles
will turn to inches
minutes... to seconds
when I can see you!

Misty eyes
no more shall be,
when you
melt into my arms.

Reminisce

The autumn came so quickly,
as if summer never happened...
my mind, warped a little
by the time flown by.

Moments separated
by experiences not shared,
although I
absolutely tried.

I reach out my arms,
my fingers outstretched,
I try to grasp what little memory
that remains.

Your boisterous laugh,
your wit and charm,
as they are captured
in my words on page.

Oh, what a treat
to have had you
in my dreams,
if just for a little while.

Where Beautiful Loves

You made me laugh
and dance and sing...
Oh, and that
Mona Lisa smile.

I realize that things
can't always stay static,
and that life deals blows
that are enigmatic.

You will always be part
of who I am now...
I carry you within
my heart,

and love you with
an unconditional love,
even when we are

apart.

Brandy Lane

It's You

I've tossed and turned
and meandered in my mind,
and cannot fathom my life
without you in it.

You are, perhaps,
one of the most
wonderful turning pages
in my existence.

You, somehow,
folded time.

You lent me your wings
when mine were broken.

You have rocked my world
down to its very core.

You are the key
to my dreams,
the palette of colors
with which I paint,
the thesaurus
with which I write.

Where Beautiful Loves

God is my salt,
but you are all of the spices...
the sweet
and the savory,
all that makes
the taste buds dance.

I have missed you tremendously.
Even in writing.
You are still with me,
always.

Brandy Lane

Unrequited

I couldn't love you any more...
I cannot love you any less
My heart beats loudly,
My brain scolds me
all in all, I'm one big mess.

How do I explain this love...

To which there's no remedy...

A love unrequited

yet unconditional

this love tween you and me?

I tuck you into someplace new...
feelings I've never known
wonderful, magical,
beautiful, closer
than family has ever shown.

You're irreplaceable, undeniable,
I cannot go without.
Trust me, I've tried...
I just about died
like a forest during a drought.

Where Beautiful Loves

I know not how to make my heart
stop aching in this way.
Unless to see you...
unless to hold you...
each and every day.

Brandy Lane

Out Loud

I cannot tell you how awful
this feeling has been...
the one where I'm not being myself,
the one where I live in a world
where I cannot write to you.

I'd rather die
than live in that agony again.

I will try to keep it slightly tame,
but hiding all of that in my heart
is like holding the seeds of exotic flowers
in a dark, dry place for safe keeping.

What is the point in having
something so precious
if we cannot enjoy its subtle fragrance
and rare beauty?

Those seeds were planted in my heart...
and they are starting to bloom.
I cannot hide it away anymore,
flowers are pouring from my heart, my soul...
my words are perfumed and colorful,
and everyone can see!

Where Beautiful Loves

It seems, in the quiet depths,
something has been building
up inside of me.
roots have formed.

And when I thought I was losing you,
my heart felt them tighten
in an effort to wake me...
in an effort to stop this silence,
so that all the world could know.

My heart is screaming to stop being quiet!

I'm so tired of
loving you in secret,
I think it's high time that
I got to love you...
out loud!

The Mighty Dragon
aka... my muse.

*where the smoke signals come from...

Thoughts flit 'round like dragonflies with nowhere to land.

Brandy Lane

If I were to run an ad...
It would simply say:

WANTED

This princess is more like a warrior than royalty.
I am through with knights who swear to protect me,
and completely done with pompous princes!

What is desperately needed is a DRAGON.
Yes, a handsome and massively brilliant dragon
would be the most welcome companion.

I would protect my dragon in exchange
for the same.
We would adventure to faraway places,
and live atop a mountain just above the clouds.

I would gaze into my dragon's hypnotic eyes,
and tell him gloriously adventuresome stories
just to see his smile.

At night, I would ask him to light a fire
(did I mention a fire breather is preferred)
and I would lie back onto his strong shoulder
and comfortably slumber.

He would wake me in the morning
with his harmonious vocalizations
and I would polish his luminous scales.
Oh! How I would care for my companion and friend!

Where Beautiful Loves

Qualifications:

*Dragons only...
no hobbits,
wizards,
warlocks
or aforementioned knights or princes.

*Fire breather with strong,
harmonious vocalization skills,
preferably with relative pitch.

*Must have strong shoulders
and a sensitive demeanor.

*Needs to love adventure,
but also love simple, quiet pleasures
and know how to find the joy in little things.

*Definitely must be a connoisseur
of the finer things,
yet realize that the finer things
aren't necessarily things at all.

If you feel that you
fit these qualifications,
please send smoke signals ASAP.

Brandy Lane

Wellspring

This wellspring of hope,
this fountain of love,
abundant and refreshing.

My lips tremble at the
mere thought of the words
that might tumble out of them,
should I cease to write them
as they come.

It would be like a geyser
should I dam them up
and not allow them
to trickle to my fingertips instead!

This intensity of emotion
within me, not wishing
to share it
with anyone other than you...
the only person I know
to understand my soul.

You are my beautiful, secret hovel...
your heart
is where I take refuge,
my home away from home.

I marvel at your hospitality,
and relish every moment

Where Beautiful Loves

as I feast on your sweetness.
More delicious than
honey from the comb
or the most decadent
of marzipan.

You fill me with everything
that brings me joy,
light,
and hope.

I'm so enamored
by your enchanting kindness,
your bountiful creativity,
your hunger for knowledge
and your playful demeanor.

You are,
perhaps,
as rare the mythical beasts
that have been
written into the expanse
of the past...
yes,
my darling,
you are definitely...

my dragon.

Brandy Lane

Fly with Me!

Gloomy dampness
and haunting gray clouds
enrobe this bedraggled day.
Oh! How I desperately need the sun
to come chase it all away!

I need a wing-ed creature
that is waterproof to fly...
high enough above the clouds,
up to the clear blue sky.

One that can soar for many mile
to where the sun doth shine,
to where the rays glint
off of the waves
of the seas of brine.

Fly with me to adventures
that will take us rather far,
from the doldrums
and the mediocrities
that this life, often mar.

Dearest dragon,
with your shiny scales
and brightest eyes of any,
I would fly with you anywhere,
let's flip a shiny penny!

Where Beautiful Loves

Heads, we go wherever I wish,
tails, you get to choose,
either way it will be fun,
as we have nothing to lose!

At night,
amongst sol's waning rays,
we'll lie next to the fire,
and tell each other our hopes
and dreams
and ethereal desires.

We'll snuggle down and cozy up
to keep each other toasty,
and I'll make you grin from ear to ear
and feed you cookies, mostly.

Oh, my friend,
you are so dear,
you're right inside my heart!
I think of you ever so fondly,
even when we're far apart.

You make me happy
just thinking of you
and adventuring
inside of my mind,
how beautiful my life is now...
one that you've helped me to find.

Brandy Lane

My Darling Dragon

Daydreaming of flying with you,
my pet,
my dear,
the holder of all of my affections.
Soaring high above the mountaintops
where the air is brisk and clear!

I wrap my arms around
your neck tightly
and whisper sweet nothing's
into your ear
and you plunge quickly
toward the valley below.

The terrain is akin
to a patchwork quilt,
with its orchards and farmlands.
In the distance,
there is a cool,
clear,
spring fed lake
where we stop to quench
our insatiable thirst.

I meander,
and gather a bit of fruit
from some nearby trees
to go along with the jerky,
nuts

Where Beautiful Loves

and bit of wine in my satchel.

We rest along the shore
as I toss apples in the air
for you to catch.

Even though you rarely speak,
time in your presence
writes volumes on its own,
as moments with you
are worth their weight in gold.

I am so very honored
to have that time with you.

I stroke alongside your snout,
toward your cheek...
and stare into your deep,
blue eyes.

Brandy Lane

I can see a whole different universe
dancing in them,
places I long to visit.

I hold your strong jaw
in my gentle hands,
as you nuzzle and grunt
as only dragons can.

You are calm
and sweet
in my presence,
but I still feel your strength,
your power,
your size over me...
but I am comforted by you,
never afraid.

I could stay with you
always,
and never grow weary of you.

My beautiful, charming beast!
I am not used
to this feeling
of how I am missing you!

Where Beautiful Loves

I am not sad that you're gone,
but more in a state of
anticipation
for the next time I get to see you!

If I begin to miss you,
I simply reminisce or daydream.
You are the most favorite being
I've ever known.

You have this magic
that surrounds you somehow,
and I always feel
as though I've found
the Fountain of Youth
after spending time
just thinking about you.

Thoughts
of your laugh,
your childlike grin,
your sparking eyes...
I cannot help but smile myself
when thinking of you.

Brandy Lane

The Greatest High

You are my resting place,
a place to catch my breath.

You are my world map,
where I go you find my bearings.

You are sinfully delicious,
and I love to steal little bites
when no one is looking.

You are my muse,
and so much inspiration
in all I do.

You have shown me
that I am beautiful,
and the reason that
I want to look my best.

You are my palette,
and my world
is no longer gray.

You are my gorgeous dragon,
the protector
of my dreams and desires.

Where Beautiful Loves

You have my heart
wherever you are...

I have missed this more
than you could even fathom.

My hands tremble
as I type the words,
knowing you are reading
my thoughts
and mind as they are written.

It's the greatest high
I've ever known.

Brandy Lane

Play with Me

Happy, dancing,
smiling, gushing...
oh, I feel
my face is flushing!

Laughing til the
tears are streaming...
oh, pinch me,
I must be dreaming!

Dearest friend,
so close to my heart...
it's heaven
when we're not apart!

I'm so happy when we get to play,
like children on a sunny day.

You make me flighty,
make me float...
I'll lower the drawbridge,
you cross the moat!

I'll call off the gargoyles
and wear a pretty dress,
but don't be misguided...
we can still make a mess!

Where Beautiful Loves

We'll make mud pies
and dragon s'mores
and write catchy tunes all day,
and I'll sit in awe and listen...
to every word you say.

I'll admire you and pray
that I make you smile,
and we can just be ourselves
for a little while.

We can stay for an hour,
or a few if you'd rather...
Heck, I'd stay all day
if reality didn't matter.

Here in our hideaway,
where no one else can see,
you can be just you,
and I can be just me.

Brandy Lane

Storytelling Dragon

I know of a mighty dragon,
who burnishes words of gold in fire...
breathes lightly cross the pages
and stories appear for all to admire!

Filled with historical facts,
delves into the past with flair...
that keeps interest of the adventurer,
whilst educating with care.

Dragons may not speak many words,
but when they write it's quite a feast!
You'll be off to a time recreated
in the mind of this magical beast!

Where Beautiful Loves

Slumbering Dragon

As I tiptoe past your slumbering dreams,
over to my chair...
I find comfort knowing that
I'm in your dragon's lair.
I start my work of writing,
as I often do,
hoping to write something
wonderful for you.
Some things are rather silly,
Some witty, cute, and smart
Some are rather loving,
they all come from my heart.
A puff of smoke emerges
from your nostril as you sleep,
and I am very careful
not to even make a peep.
I watch you in amazement
as your chest heaves up and down,
Breathing like a freight train,
At least that's how it sounds.
I watch your scale's opalesce
in the morning light,
and pray you slept as soundly
all throughout the night.
You really are magnificent,
all piled up in a heap...
and I could stay here all day long
and watch you while you sleep.

Brandy Lane

Perspective

I climb up the forbidden path,
rocky and dangerous
from the recent earthquakes.
Carefully, I check my footing...
so as not to slip and fall.

Large boulders balance,
precariously above me,
I take notice to knock them down
as I continue my ascent,
clearing the path for future visits.

I reach the top, and here you sit...
looking a bit bewildered at my return.
For all of the rubble
I had to stumble through,
our cave is seemingly pristine!

You must have been here often,
seeing as you can just fly up here
whenever you desire!

I must apologize for my detour,
as I had gotten lost along the way...
but I'm here now,
a bit bedraggled, humbled,
more timid than usual,
not quite my warrior self.

Where Beautiful Loves

Hopefully my strength will return,
after a quiet rest here...
at the only place
I know to be home.

You can see kingdoms
from way up here,
now that the clouds
have dissolved!

Looking down,
it seems chaotic,
but so easy to get sucked into
the life below.

I guess this is
my dose of perspective,
because sometimes
you are so close to something
that you can no longer recognize
what you are even peering at anymore.

I'm coming in,
you've lit the fire
and I've brought the water for tea...
I've missed coming here,
If you don't mind,
I'd just like to sit for a while in your company...
... and just be.

Brandy Lane

Wishes

Oh why can't we be
as little children and play in the sun?
I miss you...
and it's not even you keeping me away.

I feel like I'm locked in the tower!
Won't my dear, sweet dragon
come and save me?

Sigh.

I wish there were wishes to be granted,
true luck in a horse's shoe...
it would be great to find
a fairy godmother
or a leprechaun
and shake them down for their powers!

All of the many dandelions
I've blown off into the wind,
the prayers of exasperation...

I am still waiting for them to be granted.

This is perhaps, the most bittersweet, most flavorful, most enlightening, most enchanting of romances that I've ever known.

Brandy Lane

Remind Him

What can you do with a flightless dragon...
one that's lost his fire?
One that's forlorn and, for his work,
has lost all his desire?

You must become the teller of tales,
that is what's required.
To make him chortle, laugh, and snort,
and feel that he's admired.

What can you give a magnificent angel
that has brought your life such light?
Whose wings are bent so that they can
no longer produce flight?

You just sit by his side and hold his hand
to get him through the night,
then wield a sword to protect him
as you carry them into the fight.

Where Beautiful Loves

You see, when I said *unconditional*

was how this love would be,
I meant come hell or high water
or whatever comes at thee.

You are my soul's companion,
I'll do anything in my power,
to remind you of your worth
in your darkest hour.

What do you do for a beautiful man
who is lying there in pain?...

You just gently remind him you love him,

again,

and again,

and again...

Brandy Lane

Jump Start

You delight me
in ways I thought
were impossible!
Just the smallest
kindnesses
have filled my soul
to the brink of flood!

You are a constant
and glorious beacon
that comforts me.

When I crawl into
bed at night,
you are my
protective dragon!
I slumber
tucked inside
your heavy…
yet velvety soft,
down laden wings.
You are strong
and tough
on the outside,
with a gloriously soft underbelly!

Where Beautiful Loves

My heart stands still
in pause
from the last time
I saw you,
until it is jump-started again
at even just the sound
of your voice.
I could listen
to the sing song
of your voice forever
and never grow weary.

Your exuberance
is contagious,
your energy
and joy
consume my being.

I am growing
increasingly
fond of you.
I can't stop myself,
and I hope you'll forgive me,
as it was never my intention.

Brandy Lane

You have ignited
a fire within me
that has me beside myself
with a passion
and zeal that I never knew
was inside of me.

You still have yet
to invite me to use
your name,
although I must admit,
I whisper it often...
as if to send you
a burst of hope
and light
along with it
as it leaves my lips.

How I wish
to steal away with you
to just cradle
your handsome face
in my hands
and look into
your beautiful eyes.

Where Beautiful Loves

You are beautifully
appreciative...
you exude grace
and kindness.

You truly make me feel
like a gorgeous,
rare butterfly
that just made her debut
from her chrysalis.

Your words
are like nectar
from the sweetest
of flowers.
They give me the strength
to fly.

I cannot write you
without beautiful,
cleansing tears
streaming down
my face.

Brandy Lane

You have become my vice,
my confidante,
my companion in my daydreams.
My gratitude for you
is unfathomable.
I am in awe.

I wish that I could spend
just a moment
in your beautiful mind.
Just to know what's in your thoughts,
although...
your smile when you see me says a lot.
You are a little like me in that respect.

Smiling around you is a given...
and I absolutely
live
for those moments.

Where Beautiful Loves

A Sweet Hiraeth

The beauty of this day
awakened me with its glorious,
beaming light, and periwinkle sky.
I'm comfortable, warm, and happy
with thoughts of you.
I dreamt the sweetest dreams
of sugary delights,
and gazing at the stars at night.

The train is roaring by,
reminding me
of the hustle
and bustle of this world...
the things man has created
to make life "easier"
have done quite the opposite
in many ways.

I prefer the quietness,
the simple,
the appreciation
of the beauty around me.

If we were together now,
I would nuzzle into your chest
and listen to your heart beat.
I'm sure it's got a rhythm all its own.

Brandy Lane

I would listen to your adventures,
as your stories only come
in rare audio versions.

I feel I've barely skimmed the prologue
of a most interesting series of novels
mixed with small snips of
well-placed comedic charm!
I'm impatiently awaiting the release
of a much-acclaimed best seller,
but seemingly, to no avail!

Everything around me is akin
to a giant game of Jenga, so to speak.
Every move must be carefully played,
or the entire tower will fall.
I am moving slowly, and with purpose...
even though all within me
wants to be reckless.
I'm reconstructing,
building bridges... not destroying.

I love writing here,
in this place that you have gifted me.
It is my favorite pastime,
as if you couldn't tell.

Where Beautiful Loves

The hours you allow me
to spend sharing with you
are truly a gift that I can both receive,
as well as give back,
decorated with personality!

You know my mind in a way
that no one else has ever seen.

It's a sweet hiraeth.

I may not write
constantly in couplets,
or have
immense ideas in iambic pentameter,
but all of my scribbles
and dabbles of prose
come from my heart,
directly to yours.

I am no Shakespeare!
I am just little old me,
writing to sweet, wonderful you,
on a gorgeous Saturday in early spring.

hiraeth
/ˈhirˌīTH/
noun (especially in the context of Wales or Welsh culture) deep longing for something, especially one's home.

About the Author

Brandy Lane has spent most of her life in Indiana, where she resides with her husband and four children. She loves music and nature, and recently started to find a new love for writing. Always looking for a silver lining, writing became her way of painting one on even the gloomiest of thoughts. She refers to these excursions as "painting with words," and is her way of taking the reader on a journey with her to the fantastical places that are in her mind. She loves to find the hope in the melancholy, and the sunshine in the storm. Her heavy use of metaphors and analogies make her writings easy to relate to, and shows a reflection of her love of music, art, literature, and fantasy.

Brandy never actually intended on writing a book, it happened quite serendipitously! She found someone she could tell anything to, and words would just melt onto the paper from her mind. Daily, she would write to him, just telling him of her ideas and notions. Mostly, they were letters of adoration, for someone who opened her eyes that she was more than that which people she had surrounded herself, had led her to believe. She gained confidence through her writing. After several months, he told her that she should be published, he really enjoyed her work, and thought others would as well. She started showing close friends and family what she had been up to.

Social media has also impacted her growth in writing, with the uses of prompts and live readings. She has gained much support within the writing communities of both Instagram and Facebook.

Facebook:
https://www.facebook.com/wherebeautifullives/

Instagram:
https://www.instagram.com/wherebeautifullives/

A Letter from the Muse

So. Now you know.

For the past few years I've been getting love letters—usually by text—and I can't really say I've minded. It might give one an ego, but it's much too late for that—I already had one.

It's led to some awkward conversations with her husband I suppose, but I can't help that. I'm just me. Chris knows who I am, and I'm sure her children do too, by now—I've been over several times. There's enough clues in this text—but I still won't sign my name here. Yet. Let a modicum of mystery remain.

Unrequited love causes the most inspiration. And the most pain.

Part of my fear is that someday I will break this fragile glass image and I will come crashing off this pedestal I've been placed on—I'll make a mistake and say something to irreparably blemish this perfect image. I think it's inevitable—no one's perfect, least of all me. If so, that might inspire another book of much angrier poetry. In the meantime, though, we might as well luxuriate in this moment and bask in the glow of happiness, however temporary it may be. Joy is ephemeral, and life doles out scant fleeting moments of it—let's enjoy them.

This is where beauty lives.

You never know who you are inspiring. I like to think that everyone has a perfect match out there somewhere. Would you act differently tomorrow if you knew someone was watching your every move and secretly in love with you?
You'd be more confident. Perhaps more generous or more loving. Perhaps more careful with your words. You'd probably be happier and laugh more. Enjoy life more.
For that is what love does.

It is within you, dear reader, to be that person for someone else. You might already be and not know it. Look around.

The greatest gifts—friendships—are often right next to us. Or within us.

There is beauty within you. Believe it.

You are where beautiful lives.

You are beautiful.

You are.

Now live it.

Brandy's Muse,
and apparently, a Dragon

www.ingramcontent.com/pod-product-compliance
Lightning Source LLC
Chambersburg PA
CBHW020906080526
44589CB00011B/461